GEORGE MILLS

The House Sails Out of Sight of Home

THE 1991 MORSE
POETRY PRIZE
 SELECTED AND
INTRODUCED BY
PHILIP BOOTH

Northeastern University Press
BOSTON

Northeastern University Press

Library of Congress Cataloging in Publication Data

Mill, George, 1919–
   The house sails out of sight of home / George Mills ; selected
and introduced by Philip Booth.
      p.   cm. —(The 1991 Morse Poetry Prize)
      ISBN 1-55553-113-X (paper)
      I. Title.   II. Series : Morse Poetry Prize ; 1991.
PS3563.I42297H6   1991
811'.54—dc20   91-24123

Designed by Ann Twombly

Composed in Weiss by The Composing Room of Michigan, Inc., Grand Rapids,
Michigan. Printed and bound by Princeton University Press, Lawrenceville, New
Jersey. The paper is Glatfelter Writer's Offset, an acid-free sheet.

MANUFACTURED IN THE UNITED STATES OF AMERICA
96   95   94   93   92   91   5   4   3   2   1

ACKNOWLEDGMENTS

Poems in this book, some in slightly different form, originally appeared in the following: *Ascent* ("Empery," reprinted by permission of *Ascent* 13, no. 1, copyright 1987 by Ascent Corporation), *Calliope* ("No One Sees the Sun in a Dream"), *Harvest* ("Calypso," "Hurricane," "Annunciation USA," "Dillinger One Through Nine"), *Stone Country* ("First Love," "Gandhi Blesses His Assassin," "The Recognizable," "By the Cemetery"), *The Texas Review* ("Island," reprinted by permission of *Contemporary New England Poetry: A Sampler*, vol. II, a special release of *The Texas Review*, copyright 1988 by Texas Press).

Contents

Introduction

Until I had read, reread, reshuffled, and reread again the manuscripts sent me by the Morse Prize Committee, and then began to winnow them, and finally chose the book that most deeply struck me, and so informed the Committee, and was told the poet's name, I had never heard of George Mills, much less read him. Only now do I know what I might well have guessed: that the author of this oddly titled book is my senior, a man whose age informs not only the originality of individual poems, but the arc they sequentially form as he has made them into a book of lifelong consequence.

The House Sails Out of Sight of Home is a book of poems that both literally and figuratively sail out (or take off) from the familiar. In substance and structure they range from the extravagantly complex to the ultimately simple. Whoever wants to figure these poems *out* (in the high school sense of that term) might best be warned that the poems in themselves are intensively figured and refigured. The figures of the book's opening poem (which demythifies a prime myth), like the figures of the early "Child's Drawing" (the last line of which gives the book its title), are typically integral to the book's wholeness. Individually, George Mills's images can be as simply familiar as "home," "father," "snow," "wind," "the sea," or even a miniature village enclosed in a breakable glass globe filled with fake snow. But such images grow increasingly complex insofar as they recur in further poems and thus prefigure ranges of still wider seeking, where images accrete symbolic value within contexts that in themselves change.

Even as metamorphic images inform the tactics of George Mills's individual poems, I see recurrence and metamorphosis as his book's strategic strengths, particularly as they imply what I take to be a Jungian sense of synchronicity. On the first reading, I thought many of the book's earlier poems distinctively odd, even self-confounding; in subsequent readings, as I gave in to the resolute flatness of the poems' rhythms and syntax, to their ambivalent images and outrageous puns, I found the oddnesses distinctly self-illuminating: poems apparently disjunctive began to reveal themselves in ways radically coherent.

Not merely to open this book, but to open one's self to its poems, is to realize that the events they enact are both individual and archetypal. In all time and no time save the present, these are the false-dawn poems of a man who has slept uneasily, being deeply in touch with the dreams and nightmares that wake him. Even as nightmare and dream have driven him inward, so do they restore him to an outer world that is daily both new and old. From inside and outside his head, out into his poems come not only the figures of fathers and sons, but gun-toting gauchos, Calypso, Gandhi, Lincoln, Dillinger, the Sphinx, Einstein, van Gogh, Mercator, and Mary. Nothing and everything is sacred in these poems. Like the absurd reality of Gary Larson's cartoons, they invert one's workaday perceptions; they are as angular in their own perceptions (and tactics) as the incomparable drawings of Saul Steinberg's *The New World*.

If Larson and Steinberg are cousins-once-removed to these poems, their ultimate great-uncle is, as their author implicitly and explicitly acknowledges, Wallace Stevens—the Wallace Stevens, say, of "The Comedian as the Letter C," "The Snow Man," and in its tones and compressions, "The Emperor of Ice-Cream." "There is nothing in life," says Stevens in one of his *Adagia*, "but what one thinks of it." George Mills's poems are both elevated by thinking and (as one of his titles tells) literally dependent on it. Philosophically less explorative and psychologically more penetrating than Stevens's, the poems of this book know, with Stevens, how dramatically an "object slightly turned" becomes "a metaphor of the object." The child who senses how "the house sails out of sight of home" has already begun to know, as Stevens came to, that "loss of faith is growth." And as the boy later follows the house over his own first horizons, he enacts what Stevens spoke and Mills inherently knows: that "Poetry is a search for the inexplicable."

For all his forebears (whether elected or genetic), George Mills is indubitably his own man, his own poet. He knows in some inmost ear that matters "apparently irreconcilable" present "the perpetual crisis / that makes it possible / to hear / beyond convention. . . ." He remembers what "a body, made subtle / by age, suddenly remembers. . . ." He feels the power of the human scream that "model daylight people" try to keep "behind glass / . . . in its silver frame." And he writes as a poet who realizes that words related by extreme necessity become "Works Breaking Out of Frames."

I first read this book of a winter dawn that was coldly peaceful. I write now in wartime. Now that the palindromic world of 1991 has come to war with itself in ways so sanitized by censorship that what looked like Video Games have become death-and-death Superbowls of Hi-Tech Statistics and Fundamentalist Atrocity, these poems that first struck me seem even more striking. Splendidly distant from Photo-Ops, Pentagon Briefings, and Sound-Bites, the integrity of this book is on its own terms a true event. Given the poet's age in this year of our failing century, it might even be said that the book is no small advent. Dangerously, comically, wisely, *The House Sails Out of Sight* returns to *words* one man's vision of how it feels, and what it may mean, to be imaginatively human.

PHILIP BOOTH
January 1991

THE HOUSE SAILS OUT OF SIGHT OF HOME

✒ Myth of the Sacred Marriage

All night long the whisperings are passed
from rib to rib.
Night with its badly kept secrets
is no time to fall asleep.

A rib wants to leave my side
and do her hair in her own way.
She wants to stand opposite me,
wearing tall black boots,
and speak my name
in a compelling voice.

I sit upright in bed,
pants empty, helpless,
tossed over a chair.
She wants to ride with me
across tomorrow's desperation,
mouths wide open, singing.

God tried to wake us with a fingertip.
She fires a revolver.
The trajectories above my head
are like cathedral arches.
I gather up my gargoyles
for a leap.

Annunciation USA

for Eilshemius

When I was a kid clouds
were good at questioning
the street's authority far below.

Their white turmoil rose
out of the trumpet vines around the house.
Mumbling clothespins, mother hardly noticed.

A cloud could hide a city where
naked butchers hacked red meat,
naked priests turned wafers into God
and naked wise men started up new storms.

One afternoon, three women,
stripped of all but summer breeze,
swept lightly past me over the lawn,
not touching down.

These things happen in out-of-the-way places.
I went to live in out-of-the-way places.
I spent my life taking off
what finally must be taken off.

Priestly

The wind around the house moans
on the verge of satisfaction.
It sounds like home out there,
sounds like the high calling
of the revolver.

The wind moans, I open the door,
am swept away.

My turned-around collar
requires me to shoot
my way through one impetuous
abstraction after another,
down to the shore of love.

Bewitching women
live at the edge
where earth slants out of sight
beneath the ocean.

I'm a priest
who easily forgets
the meaning of mass
and keeps bending his knees,
trying to remember.

Pearlhandles flecked
with sunlight and salt,
I chase women,
trying to remember.

🌿 Free Acts

The computer screen lights up.
So do hairtrigger eyes

in love
with the suspense

of purposeless acts.
I've pushed many an old man

off the speeding train.
—There he goes,

he's falling falling
but hasn't hit the ground—

just time for a haiku yell.
Now he's out ahead

of his name, out where
the weightlessness

begins. His birthmark
bursts into flame,

a routine part
of our abandonment

on the doorstep of fire,
on the verge of language,

mouth of wet ashes.
This must be why

my wife, arms full
of groceries,

kicks shut the door
and for no reason at all

bends down
and gives me a kiss.

⚜ *Private Eye*

It's not easy to be a private eye,
following a woman, coming alive
for both our sakes in shadow after shadow,
bringing darkness up into the light.

The last one was a stranger on a bus.
I looked at her: renunciation flared,
gaudier than pleasure and passion.
Remember that she must not

know how close behind
I am, caring for nothing
but the work: her happiness,
my anonymity.

I show her how to wreck
the world of clothes
and strip off nakedness.
The night that she blows out

the candles on the cake
of secret joy,
all of them with one breath,
that night we sleep together.

When morning comes, the names of things
leap transparent into light.
It's a model world—windless, motionless.
One touch will set it going.

⚜ *Meditation*

The morning sun sieves down
through my pores into that city
mystics know but cannot build.
It's a day to roam there,
checking the hiding place under the tongue,
the bearings of the fist,
those oily sapphires.

A day to check the heart,
knotted on itself, the half-lotus heart,
busy counting every breath.
The wall that splits the heart
is chalked over with the count.

The statue of mother,
now she's dead, has a diamond
set in the curve of her nose.
I touch it for luck—
hang skeins of my blood
between her outstretched hands
and roll them in a ball.

Full of the momentum of laughter
I run right off my morning cheek
and hang suspended with the storm
around the stillness of the eye.

All goes well in midair
until I look down.
Meditation has no bottom.

Tattoo

He is alone now,
well into the desert.
He stops the car, gets out,
takes off his shirt.

It's a small tattoo.
He shows it to the sky,
itself the outcome
of a youthful escapade.

Snowman and Girl

The threatening sky itself
turns into snow,

each flake unique,
and falls.

We hear it in the dark,
a white unbroken world

moving through our own
to be there in the morning,

centered on a man of snow.
The child next to him

seems far away,
almost at the vanishing point.

Even so we hear her clearly
as she turns to him

and speaks her name out loud.
Her name, carefully enunciated,

amuses her.
She laughs.

She says it again.
It sounds like an alias.

This time the wind
blows it away.

She reaches out to touch
the man of snow.

Love of a snowman
has her hands in mittens.

Snow Globe Village

The streets crook back to medieval times.
Smoke at dawn swirls off into wet woods.
Trees with bad backs glide in and out
of sleep. Sleep is much too clever
for a simple fellow, and waking
is not my best state.
All that tap tapping inside,
as if I were the blind man
of snow globe village.

A boy sits up late stroking
his palm's mountain of Venus.
A woman plays solitaire with kings
who have two heads.
An old man at the edge of town,
stretched out in the dark,
is saving up his little blackouts.
The wind is like a distant crowd
swearing one of history's oaths.

It's autumn in snow globe village.
Nothing has been proved all over again.
Except we sing on Sunday mornings,
and singing, if contained
and made intense enough,
will burst a small space.

Huge Crime

When morning came I had to guess
what lay under each snow shape.
The sun burst in, throwing me back
to the world's beginning.
Snow light everywhere, the green
glass pitcher cheered,
my fingertips tingled.

There's a woman who dreams
of making us rich
by robbing snow banks.
She sandpapers her fingertips,
making them sensitive
to the fall of tumblers
inside the white locks.
I still remember how I woke to find
the muddy yard transformed.
Huge crime is possible.

In the meantime, we live with muddy yards
and ink our fingertips
and keep the prints on file
for prosecuting minor thefts.

First Love

She had climbed too high.
He felt the fear that is everywhere.
What sometimes happens to trees
putting out the topmost apples
happened to them.
The two of them
high up together
grew very quiet,
held each other close.

Others came.
Each in turn
took her in his hands
and passed her down
to the next man.
They passed her down
from man to man
until she stood on earth again.
Without a word
she headed home.

Lying sometimes under a tree
he feels the giving in his hands.
All around him blades of grass
reach up.

Love Poem for a Stranger

Love is silent barter.
Our bodies, joined,

are the stone in the clearing.
You set your gift there

and go back to the city.
I take your gift

and retreat to my woods.
We never meet.

This flower is for you—
thunder under every petal.

Hurricane

You row your boat
through the drowned woods
to grandma's house, anchored
in midstream.

Your rowboat, tied up,
longs for salt waves.
It longs for the ocean,
but is afraid.

Grandma wants her snapshot
taken beside the helm.
Her goldbraid shimmers
along the wall.

The day is hot
but you try on the cloak
that matches your red hair
and swirl in place.

Outside you glimpse the wolf
raging on the bank.
He can't stand water
or a story that goes wrong.

At lunch, the cold
of a summer day
cuts into you
with a shiver.

✒ The Black and White Garden

Think of a labyrinth, a rigorous mosaic
of longstemmed blacks and whites,
a grave queen moving down its alleys.

Victorians arranged this garden
so a man and a woman in a secluded corner,
having brought lunch in a basket

and spread out a large piece of flannel,
could sit facing each other
and slash their wrists in private.

The unclean spectacle of blue blood
gasping for air and spurting out red
altered the theory of gardens.

Still, no one notices the caterpillar,
distinguished and aloof in dark glasses,
gardening on a thousand legs.

Child's Drawing

The house is a ship.
Before all that sky at the windows
daddy stands straight
like a big wooden steering wheel.
Sometimes he calls me his goldbraid
and holds me close.
A door slams down below.
No words come up only the anger.
An anchor raised.

The house sails out of sight of home.

No One Sees the Sun in a Dream

He has the dream down to one person.
One man, one moon.

He has the notion darkness
is a liberating color.

He's out in the boat for a close look.
This is the dream of the close look.

His eyes absorb the darkness
of a rogue sun.

Tick tick: the marrow clock.
He rows

as toward a diagram
of what's missing.

As toward a cup
of neighbor's light.

By the Cemetery

At the end of the sea wind's long sweep
a kite high up.
The same wind tilted
the gravestones.

The dead hold
onto their names—
Towler, Serpa, Shane.
The dead are

famous as grass.
Light slides down
the long sagging string.
It throbs, it tugs at my hand.

Calypso

How does it feel, emerging
from a log to be worshipped?
How does that shift from faceless wooden power
to being Woman feel?
With the hips and breasts
of a goddess on a Hindu temple
it's no wonder you got shipwrecked
with that sailor.
When the sea is rough, he hugs and kisses you.
He paws his prayers all over you.
Women are more buoyant than men.

Ushnishasitatapatraparajita: what a nickname!
He coos it in your ear, blowing up
the vowels like water wings.
It sounds like up-on-the-crest-down-in-the-trough.
Thank you, Gorgeous, he says.
What for? you say.
The moment just passed, he says.
How is he to know the other half of your log
was made into a hog trough?
You drift along together,
Calypso and Bentley,
both half drowned.

The Invention of Xmas

Pan is dead. So is Arthur.
God the Father and Santa Claus are dead.
Once a year Santa tries for a comeback.
Maybe down an obscure street
someone young enough for awe
is trying out, on his body,
the wounds that precede holy days.

Take that palm tree Wallace Stevens stumbled on.
At the end of the mind beyond the last thought
it stands rooted in the earth.
A firefangled bird devoid of human meaning,
human feeling, roosts there.
Easily startled, it may fly away
to nest in the bestiary of poets.

The Chinese not only named the Ten Thousand Things
that spill over us, belching
and farting like the sea;
they also noted the skills and pleasures
of life upon the waves.

Laughter up till now has been tentative and passive.
I'm working on a new brand.
Here's an example: I break my leg
and the bone jags out,
whiter than my underwear.
I begin to laugh.
The paramedic doesn't.

🪶 The Recognizable

A man writes his life
into the pages of a letter.
The tide falls,
the sky comes down,
earth stands ready
to sustain an immensity
of darkness.
Leaning into the lamplight
he licks a stamp
and fixes to one corner
of the envelope
a face
familiar to us all.

❧ Quest

A man goes looking for the right woman.
It begins in the crib at night—headlights
of the approaching moment startle him.
Fatfingered, he tries to poke a hole
in water. Later with a paddle,
he succeeds: small whirlpools out behind.
And so the girl next door showed my son
the leaves but not the sunlight
sucked down. He almost drowned
in her. Man to man, one morning,
we shook hands, he paddled off.
Small islands endlessly out front.
Sweat mixed with spray as he dug in,
hips stationary under thrusting arms.
A man looking for the right woman tries
one more river bend, skirts one more falls.
Then he's back—loud overhead.
My son home from Africa, unchanged
except for a few stories
and the knickknacks on his windowsill.

Poem That Depends Entirely on Its Title

When we enter it, swearing at our gear,
the wilderness moves off a little way.

Humus, like a carpet with a pattern,
a mind of its own, runs on, leading us,

we're sure, where no person has been.
There we will set down the known.

Leaves fall. No matter how they change,
leaves are the color of high seriousness.

Birds fly south. Leperwhite, snow comes.
It storms up so high, nothing reaches

earth. I think of my father long dead.
I love him, wherever he is, out ahead,

with everything he needs on his back.
A tribe we meet trails strings among the trees,

looking for a way out. Upturned,
their faces are a net beneath those cries

the forest stretches taut against the sky.
Blood narrows at the wrist like white water

they say *and we want out.* We sign back
the stones shall not have not lived in vain.

That Things Are the Same There as Here

The father keeps dipping out
the mirror's cold water.
He wants the images of longing,
pain and rage to be clear.
These images do not belong to him

but come from down below.
The son, when no one watches,
opens a hand and studies it.
The hand surprises him.
It's his and no one else's—
his hand split painfully to fingers.

The father takes his son to the shore.
Together they build a castle.
The son learns how to make himself small
and cross the drawbridge of the castle.
Hurry, father says, and meet the Queen
before the next wave comes.

There beside the sea,
waiting for his son's return,
the father opens his fist.
His grasp on nothing
grows less violent.

Son and Father

I try to show the old man
how light slips under islands,

lifts them off the waves—
try to make him feel the promise.

Home from school one afternoon
I pass a hoop around home.

Dad understands. Smiling,
without a word, he upends

my snow globe village
and leaves the room.

I stoop to watch the storm
down every street

and feel how snug it is
from room to room

inside the houses.
One cold day years later

it comes back—
how deliberately

my father left me there
absorbed in a toy.

Eyes

These eyes have nothing to get out
of bed for. Lazy eyes,

full of hazel lights, suspended
in the ocean of the streams of story.

They know how cold it is up high
where the unsmiling row of fathers

moves slowly out of sight
into a tradition without faces.

Eyes that are prepared to whirl
and face a landscape of armies.

They will not miss the wild joy
in the faces coming to extinguish them.

Illusion

It sinks out of sight,
has no place to go
but into the body
with other things
tagged to be lost.

When nothing is all
I have, nothing
is not enough.
I throw it away
and buy a ticket.

The bus is about to start.
Through my seethrough face
on the window
I watch emotion
filled goodbyes.

Parrot

Organs, like planets,
go round and round
the body cavity.

What they circle
has to be flamboyant.

Moonlit nights you hear
the ritual hum
toned down.

So many airborne cries
to push along out front
I need the help
of an orange and green parrot.

No flying, just sage iridescence
in place upon its perch.

Swept Away

Suppose there's love in a story.
Not love the crown
but love the keel—
the ship is in dark water.

Suppose it's the story
of love the leaf
seesawing down below the surface,
its delicate veins
gradually extinguished.

You follow the story down
because it's yours.
You hang suspended
in the murky green.
You must know how it ends.

Up above, those who care
are peering down
over the side of a narrow boat.
You can just make out
their anxious gargoyle faces
blurred by the wind.

Wave back, wave back.

✺ Gaucho

A prehensile hand, with nervous gesture,
reaches down, unzips the pampas
and the cowboy sperm.

Language invented this hand.
Language has grown impossible to live with
since the Diamond Sutra.

Language may be right, though.
A hand in bed quickly outgrows the bedroom,
takes off across the pampas

to become an epic hand
only pampas can contain.
Language once put big names like Life

and Vice Versa into circulation
but found they're too effeminate
even for a woman.

Now a pigeon out of the clouds
brings a message from Captain Hand.
He found cowboys inside a wooden horse

breathing fetid air.
They call themselves heroes he says.
Who knows where the pampas end?

I interviewed a hero once.
Life in camp had made him hazy
about the nomenclature of woman.

Crossing the Rio Bravo he squealed
when the green cold water
hit his privates.

Gandhi Blesses His Assassin

He has no trouble finding his assassin
in the crowd.

They face each other like lions
in front of a library.

Curses and blessings fly through air
and lodge in flesh,

bullets crazy for a home.
As in a mirror, Gandhi raises his right hand,

the assassin his left. They pull
the trigger together.

Dillinger One through Nine

1

An aimless kid at the county fair
paints his cartoon thought on a balloon
and lets it go,
just to watch the heads tilt back.

2

Later, his revolver becomes the iridescence
that no one possesses—the catalyst
transforming people's lives,
itself unchanged.
Dillinger, the transcendental.

3

He sways down the street
as inconspicuous as a woman in labor.
Every safe deposit box contains a fetus.

4

The mirror is as far as most of us go
before turning back.
Dillinger keeps on.

5

He's filming a bank robbery.
No, he's robbing the bank.
He lets us think he's making a film.
You want to try out for the leading role.

6

He's a whittler. Got it from his farmer father.
He likes to carve long balsa chains.
At night he dresses up in them.

7
He shakes hands like a Rotarian.

8
Dillinger has this to say: the one
who shoots me dead will kill himself
because of me.

9
He's dying in your alley.
Wipe the blood off his lips.
Keep the Kleenex in your vault. A relic.

The Late Great

My grandfather said a newsboy
was shouting *Lincoln shot.*
Instead of pocketing the four ball
he upended his bourbon, combed
his hair in the mirror, and left.
You might say it's become
a family tradition.

Let's run the film one more time,
each gesture prolonged, examined.
The president is smiling, waving.
You can't see the bullet racing up its arc,
but when it catches him, his head jerks back.
The faces in the crowd are startled—mouths
ripped open by their cries.
Grown old with repetition, the bullet
does not die.
It hits the mark—slow and ceremonious.

The story veers off into the fabulous,
taking the bullet with it.
My eyes were moving up my arm.
You know the way the eyes creep up
as high as they can go and linger there.
A little higher and you vanish into yourself.
People ask where were you when it happened.
That's where I was—halfway up my arm.

✳ Gettysburg

The bearded man thinks we're too mature
a species

To be shot at by our own kind. He moves on,
one of

The wavering line of them. They have
crossed

The stone wall. The young one leaped it
with a shout.

They straighten their line, seem to breathe
more deeply

Now they're in the open. I almost understand,
almost fall

With them into extremity, glance for re-
assurance

At the man beside me, hear my name called
from up

The line, the loving jeer of my name,
the clank

Of metal. The line sweeps on past
stricken

Heaps and puffs of smoke like the small
round

Tables where we sit with coffee cups,
squeezing

Close together, posing for one more
grinning

Snapshot of the immobility of the world
and its alibi.

Lincoln

Snow hisses among the buckeye trees.
For no reason at all, he shouts
and tosses his cap in the air.

Unusual compassions come with the hormones—
like having to go back
and help a mudholed pig.

There are law cases and funny stories
to get right.
With his bride he buys a horsehair sofa.

It's late at night, he walks the corridor.
He must write down his dream
—both sides may lose.

For no reason at all, sharpening a quill,
he's back there with the snowflakes,
shouting.

In the photo taken shortly before
he died, he seems to be waiting
for his cap to come down.

✍ Empery

The Queen's horse,
when it shits,
opens like a timelapse rose.

On almost any day her African sunlight
upends itself
and pours out lions.

She has a house snake
for thinking thoughts
beyond the human mind.

Or take her pet ostrich:
its eyeballs weigh
more than its brain,

Its gizzard
is full
of uncut diamonds.

That goat circling
the expensive vase
is half man—

Yes, and royal admiration notes
the longevity
of the erection.

And then one day
—most notable
of all—

The Queen's puppy
comes out from under
her skirt,

Sits whimpering between
her body
and her severed head.

Graduate students in the great
library of Alexandria made love
in the remote stacks.

For a long time the true arch rose
between Shakespeare's thighs,
the heavy keystone locked in place.

God regroins the dust
to match what Einstein had in mind.
Already we've had enough of Einstein.

The librarian keeps a close watch.
White knuckles grip her rubber stamp.
Life is terrifying, she prefers culture.

She goes home at night, has a little
supper by herself and then lies down
across her bed and sobs.

How the Buddha to Come Will Get His Start

He crawls around under the table.
Pausing by a favorite pair of well-shaved calves,
he sends a drawing to the upper world—
    little fish devouring the big.

A report comes back so glowing
with the raw materials of sun and moon,
he shoves a second sketch up to the light—
    strongbox with the key locked up inside.

By now the thighs to which these supplications
are addressed, caryatids straddling
felicitous abysses, strongholds
odorous with peril, have raised

The flag of his young soul about to grow
a country complete with war, sickness,
death and the latest news of growing old.
Nubile telephones aroused from booth to booth
across the land whisper *pipsissewa pipsissewa*.

✒ Fundamentalist

Imagine his surprise when he heard the Sphinx
shout *wrong wrong wrong.*
She grinned too, the bitch.
He expected her blow
to knock him off the cliff.
It came more like a caress.
She studied him.
Your eyes are too close together she said.
You've been focusing too narrowly,
too intently, for too long.
Her smile was disarming.
I'm going to give you another chance she said.
We'll roll the dice. I mean dice with pips
that fume and glower and condemn.
I don't understand he said.
We'll use your eyeballs for dice she said.
Dice are square he said.
Your eyeballs are square enough she said.
While she guffawed, he kneeled
and improvised a prayer
to the calculus of divine probability.
Trying not to show repugnance,
he took his slimy eyeballs in one hand
and made as if to rattle them.
You rolled snake eyes. She laughed.
You're the best blind date I've ever had.
Then she got serious.
Beat it. I've done enough for you.
He scoured the horizon with his daughter's eyes,
the only eyes he had, thanks to the Sphinx.
What is it he said, repeating her riddle,
that goes on four legs in the morning,
two at noon, and three in the evening?

42

His Stone

Sometimes with effort
he lifts the stone
onto his shoulder,
takes it for a ride.
Love and the spiral
have much in common.
Or the stone is a pitcher
on top of his head
and he a woman,
graceful at the well.
A stone crowded with numbers,
easily mistaken for a head.

The valley loves his dropping in
for breakfast.
His hobby is to count the leaves
on trees, the waves on water.
He has memorized the lists
and patterns of the stars.
He tabulates young girls.
Should he for a moment
not look below their darling throats
he might grow old.
The scandal of our lives,
as he discusses it,
keeps us laughing
throughout breakfast.

Up on the mountain
it's the wizardry of clouds
that seethe and writhe
and tower upward.
Shading his eyes,

he follows their ascension.
It seems so easy then
to lift the stone,
lift it overhead
and leave it there
secure on top.

⚜ *Wafer*

His infallible recipe, bleached and shrunk
to wafers stamped out by a machine—
that's what's left of God.
The wine on the altar shivers,
knowing what's to come.

Mary, now that the church is empty,
touches a finger to her lips
and unbuttons her blouse. Smiling,
she holds out each cancerous breast in turn.
Stepping down from her niche,

she stands before the altar.
At her signal, the Bull God is led in.
Mary runs her thumb along the sacrificial blade.
She works skillfully, hoisting her skirt
so the blood spurts over her thighs.

✍ *Sullivan*

The heritage of battle
lodged in his side
made him asymmetrical.
He rose

As to a flyby cloud,
called out for centuries
of help
and got it.

Having frayed himself like a flag
in the history of the world,
he turned to friendlier abysses
not wide enough

To fall into.
He read his favorite book
for the last time,
ripping out each page.

Some say they lost him
in an avalanche of light
as sun leaned in
and burned the toast.

Others glimpsed him
at the top of stairs
that go nowhere, waiting
to have his passport stamped.

He had tasted the spoon,
the way it keeps back nothing
for itself
and it drove him crazy.

Whoever paints a pattern
on a paper bag,
sticks in his head and hollers,
honors Sullivan.

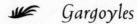 *Gargoyles*

We no longer look up
when the gargoyles howl
and gibber at the neighbors.

Or when they lean far out,
one arm around the cross,
to peer down the fronts

Of women's dresses.
Gargoyles are the town's historians.
They see through curtains.

Like the time mom walked in
and us two kids
kept right on.

✺ Man Dead

Here is a mirror.
In it the man practiced his variations,
expecting some inadvertent event
to set things right.

Here is a street.
It stared up at the crotches
of soldiers, privileged by a badge
to force open doors.

Believe me, the mirror would rather
be draped with a towel
than have to repeat
what went on out there.

Here are foul words the young woman
scrawled across the mirror with lipstick.
She lies on the bed, one hand fallen to the floor.
No surgeon will take out love and fix it.

There, across the room,
is an old woman, the man's mother,
making islands out of white of egg
and floating them on seas of custard.

The mirror catches a corner
of the sky, smooth
as the mirror
but without its backing.

Urspeak

Words keep back a little fun
A little sorrow for themselves

You speak them and they are gone
They have their own lives to live

Where is home for *stone* and *cup* and *door*
There in the distance

Nothing interrupts the light
Words arrange themselves like things

That cast no shadows
Death is fascinated

By our shadows
It creeps in close to watch

For it I make the beaks and snouts
Of birds and animals against the wall

Seaside Town

Towns like this build
ocean-goers out of stray males.

Trailing bottles in brown bags
and parts of widows

like abandoned yellow school buses,
an ocean-goer has no

motor, rudder, ballast.
There's a wide selection of sad songs

to sing while this goes on—
if you feel sad.

You lie down in a wave's hollow
and set your head beside you

on a foamy rack.
Your head floats off.

The men who build real boats
are sure to gather on the shore

and wave as you go by.
If only you could paint

the name of your homeport
across the stern.

⊱ White Xmas

Some day I hope to step
out of the closet and become
a white xmas dropping
onto people's heads.
Let's say an old man
shoveling fairyland aside
has a thanatotic
seizure. I'm a killer,
I get into the headlines.
I'm fingerprinted. Letters
to the editor demand
a trial. A writer wants
to do my story but not
until he gets an advance.
Bishops pray for me.
A psychiatrist concludes
that pain on xmas day
is just the right size.

I want to be the kind
of white that leaves no dirty
prints behind, the white
black envies. Death row
will feel twinges as I
pass over. Some thinktank genius,
up all night, will try
to stuff me back inside
my atom. My plump effigy
ought to grace one front yard
after another. Kids
will take me for a model,
give me dad's best pipe
to smoke . . .

The Mask of Myself

That man caught in the mirror
is the man after my own heart,
face indistinguishable from the ravenous
lights and shadows making it up.

All because he overdid
the way one overdoes
when it's time to be born.

Occasionally he leaves the house
and hugs an oak as if to learn
how to stand still
among simple variations of sky.

Back home he overdoes
the way one overdoes
until it's time to die.

Works Breaking Out of Frames

Take the wine-dry milk of a Rivelli Virgin.
The Jesus at her breast
will become the Christ all right
but with a flaw. When tired, he will lapse
into a good-year-bad-year, glass-clinker lingo,
too refined for the apostles.

Rivelli's walls hunker down like gnomes
with cracked mouths whispering madonna madonna
at every woman who passes.
Rivelli always includes a flea,
half hidden on the Virgin's brocade—
a mescaline-induced elf flea, overdressed in wings,
specializing in angelic dirty work.

Rivelli catapults me back to East Cleveland
and that virgin aunt
who used to brush my cheek
with an acid-flower mouth.
She would finger my shirtsleeve and say,
"Eating, my boy, is a dark enterprise. Make sure
you do it alone."
I knew her better than the others did.
I think Rivelli's more-than-flea
hovered near her ear that day
and whispered, "You are with God."

The chances are good that halfway down
between the bridge and river,
primly falling,
aunty changed her mind.

ᴗᴇ Mercator and van Gogh

One morning the young Mercator glimpses
his sister's naked breasts crisscrossed
with latitudes and longitudes.
He sees how the surface of a globe
can be spread out in two dimensions.
He sees a way to map a sphere.
That same morning he finds a comb in the street
and starts his hair on a new life.

He watches his family, one by one,
come down the stairs to breakfast;
one by one, go stumbling up at night.
His indifferent father
passes him in the hall.
Mercator vows to pin
the hide of the world
above his bureau.

He buys a knife, the kind that folds its sharp
edge in.
He splays a hand against his bedroom wall
and scores its outline there,
then leaves his father's house for good.
Home is on some other projection.

There's a longitude that runs
from Belgium down to Arles.
Someone is walking along it.
He looks like an escaped convict.
He looks like a Christian, late for martyrdom.
He walks the longitude like a drunk,
proving he's sober.

Van Gogh likes to paint a woman in one sitting.
Skimming the sky off some other world,

he sets it down around her for size.
Mme. Roulin, the postman's wife,
massive in her chair, staring back,
fills him with serenity.

One day he overhears his knife
admiring rope's ability to hang a man.
He wants to kick his famous yellow chair
out from under him.
Instantaneous masterpiece!

He spends some time trying to paint Mercator's
longstemmed beauties, his longitudes,
blooming white at the poles,
but the bouquet, the still life,
won't stay propped.

✒ My Friend, the Countess Maxima

Most of the time I don't have much fun.
The rest of the time I don't have any.
I said that once to make her laugh.
Her only comment was: you freak!
A good example of her wit.
You want to know why I'm close
to the Countess Maxima?
Vasquez was painting her one day—
a sketch the two of them
could joke about in private.
He needed a head
to balance her naked ass.
She called me in.
I think he did my touch of ugliness
better than her beauty.
She took a liking to me.
Wanted me to hang around.
Said she liked the way I made the right mistakes.
I said her rules of beauty were too strict for me.
I fell in love.
I call her Max, mostly to annoy her.
I have my own rules—
the rules of the painting.
I lift my head three inches
and everything inside the gilt frame shifts.
I know my place.
She'd love to forget hers.
I spit on fun.
Because I have that kind of job to do.
You've probably guessed that I'm a dwarf.
I've passed my test.
I'm an aristocrat.
My lady dreads the thought.

She dreads the naked truth.
Why did I lie?
Lying is what freaks are all about.
Besides, I didn't lie.
I just didn't tell you.

﹏ Henri Rousseau Rambles On

A friend told me I'd lost my handle
on reality, then I lost my glasses,
both in the same morning.
My wife is good on reality
but the glasses haven't turned up.
That leaves a tiger in midair.
Anyway, I've had enough of jungles
for a while. A Paris suburb's next—
a lake well stocked with fish,
some houses and a road that just
hangs around. That's my kind of road.
I'm good at making trees look like
the innocents they are. I may include
myself in a funny broadbrimmed hat.
No one works in my paintings.
We fish. We dangle lines all day.
See, over there, how the woman's
roundness, the boat's, echo each
other. Move that white parasol
left a little and you have a button—
road and lake and sky buttoned together.
As for the girls busy making faces
behind the man in black, I think
their giggles rate a flawless sky.

Driven in by the snow, he hesitates,
unsure of this place,
then stamps the snow off his feet
and makes his way to the corner
where the stained diaries of men in pith helmets
are shelved.
He takes off one overcoat.
The second makes him feel safe.
He begins to doze.

For the kid hunched over the table next to him,
no writers exist.
The great poems are too porous.
Half lit by the lamp, the kid grows tense.
He's figuring out a way
to swim up the page
against the current of fine phrases
in search of home.

The millennium is coming to an end.
Placed side by side by the Dewey decimal system,
the tiger and the lamb wait
to clear their throats and sing.

Nothing by Accident

The invisibility of the wind
is a kind of triumph
over counting

The invisibility of light
is more like blood
spilled on a stone

I've seen the dark
waiting in a mirror
for the next bus

I lived most
of my life
without a hero

Along came a tree
with leaves
that fall off

Palabra

The Spanish poem is an apparition
wearing spurs.
A flame juts up out of its skull
as it clangs into church
where candles aren't noticed.
This corpse, dressed in history's
gorgeous rags, seizes your lapel,
tells you how to walk
the precipice of bread,
how to call the flesh's bluff.
Its fetid breath streams over you,
incense of love.
Put your arms around it,
hug it close—
be the bloodred surf
beating on its bonewhite shore.

The Scream

Better to keep it behind glass.
Better to keep it in its silver frame
alongside the snapshot of mother.

Mother is the one dangling
her favorite outburst
between thumb and forefinger,
twirling it to teardrop shape.

When no one was around
I'd take it off the mantel,
run my finger down the glass
and smear the power on myself.

Model daylight people, listen—

Is there still that pause
at the top of each breath,
an untried road stretching away
but only for an instant?

Going to Persia

A body, made subtle
by age, suddenly remembers, says it out
to no one in particular

and then with paper cup for guide,
not spilling a drop,
walks down the corridor

out to where blossoms, splashed
against a brick wall,
grow down instead of up, grow small.

A body, made subtle, grows smaller too.
It's surprised to find how little
dinners and dialogs have become.

Persia did it: the King,
distressed by strife,
stepped into his favorite miniature.

He asked a tiny bird
where in the world he might find
a place of kindly sentiments.

Minuscule, almost out of sight of his retainers . . .
The court psychiatrist insists
the King has gone too far.

🌿 Poemska

As when a bellhop
in red uniform
has been strapped
to a fish
as large as he is
and both are inserted
in a painting
no one else can enter
There they are
apparently irreconcilable
as if put there
by some story
not quite ready
to be told
This is the perpetual crisis
that makes it possible
to hear
beyond convention
that nameless voice
whose urgency
repeated every day
at unexpected moments
grows more meaningless
more loved

Autumn Swans

In summer they slip across the lake
using one foot. That innocent look.
At lunch, they poke their scuts at the sky.
Their black masks are never askew.
They match the first snow of fall,
white for white. Summer has failed
to thaw their hearts. Summer is over.
Fierce-eyed in the first light, a fever
of uneasiness—wings lash water
and they rise. High up the sky is lighter.
Two lines fan out, we hear their voices.
We follow them with upturned faces.
The swans have left earth and its rules
behind. Suffering is for fools.

ᾧ Madbread

Everyone is sure his life
is one of those designed
to be scanned
not lived
the pain is so great.

Babies
set down in their cribs
are expected to cry softly
in the midst
of unbearable iridescences.

Christ comes
to the pious old woman
begging to be crucified.
Go away she says
I don't have the strength.

Home is where
you're most apt to be beaten,
raped, jackrolled.
Home is where
you check your credibility

first thing on waking.
No one is kicked out.
No one is to blame.
No one is much help.
The old man in a rage

leaves a few things unsaid
out of love.
It's hopeless but not serious.
Exorbitant morning
I am your exorbitant man.

Island

The moon among the clouds does her Australian crawl.
She towed us out to sea one night
and cut us loose.
The sea has thought us out.

Few here practice the world out loud.
Fishermen boot up each morning, work a common grave.
The rest of us cross legs, wrap hands around hot mugs,
exactitude enough.

Yesterday I watched a halfnaked kid come riding in
on the island's white wake.
He shouted his big shout.
This far out who cares.

At night beyond the reach of human ears
ants in the walls perfect their smallness.
The silent work of salt goes on.
We drift across the opulent waste.

A NOTE ON THE AUTHOR

George Mills was born in East Cleveland, Ohio, in 1919, and educated at Dartmouth College and Harvard University. He taught cultural anthropology for a time but gave it up for kinds of work that left him more time to write. He has flown B-17s and worked in an arts center, for a printer, for a landscaper, and for a pipe-organ builder. He is married to a wise woman who only occasionally threatens to reveal what it's like to live with a writer. Many years ago he decided that poets know something the rest of us do not. He's doing his best to discover what poets know.

A NOTE ON THE PRIZE

The Samuel French Morse Poetry Prize was established in 1983 by the Northeastern University Department of English in order to honor Professor Morse's distinguished career as teacher, scholar, and poet. The members of the prize committee are Francis C. Blessington, Joseph deRoche, Victor Howes, Stuart Peterfreund, and Guy Rotella.